Real Estate Investing:

Master the Skill of Real Estate Investing

Kris Roberts

Additionally, the information in the following pages is intended only for informational purposes and should thus be thought of as universal. As befitting its nature, it is presented without assurance regarding its prolonged validity or interim quality. Trademarks that are mentioned are done without written consent and can in no way be considered an endorsement from the trademark holder.

Table of Contents

Introduction

Congratulations on purchasing *Real Estate Investing: Master the Skill of Real Estate Investing* and thank you for doing so. This book is going to provide you with all of the knowledge that you need to begin earning money through the avenue of real estate investing. Unlike becoming a real estate agent, real estate investing is a bit different in the sense that you are truly given the opportunity to be your own boss. Of course, there are good and bad aspects that come with this responsibility, but after you've gotten through the initial learning curve, you'll be well on your way to earning passive income in an exciting, sometimes risky, and overall rewarding field. You may feel like you're not yet prepared to invest in real estate for the simple fact that you don't know where to start or how much money you need. This book will provide you with all of those details, plus more. Would it comfort you to know that many success real estate investors begin their real estate investment journey with little to nothing in terms of tangible real estate investment experience? If you prepare yourself in advance through the study of this field, you'll be better able to tackle any and all obstacles that you find along the way. You've taken the first step towards your investment future by purchasing this book. This is only the beginning, and your path to success will only become clearer from here.

The following chapters will discuss many aspects of the real estate investment process. These topics will include information regarding the typical mistakes that beginner real estate investors make and how you can seek to avoid them, how you should be organizing yourself financially, and will even provide you with actionable strategies that you can begin to take as a real estate investor. Additionally, there are many different types of real estate investing that you can research and begin to become well acquainted with. This book will take you through the ins and outs of how to invest in each one, including commercial real estate, real estate investment groups, real estate investment trusts, and even how to become a good landlord if you are interested in renting out a home to some tenants. All of these different types of real estate investing require hard work and a commitment to a certain type of organization. If you invest your money in the proper channels, you'll be able to not only realize which type of real estate investment strategy is the best for your personal style and psyche; you'll also be able to diversify your portfolio to include different types of investments once you become well versed in one type. It could take years before you know exactly what you need to do time and again in order to invest in successful real estate properties, but after reading this book you will have a basic understanding of exactly what you need to do in order to get started within each field. Often, once you get over a certain obstacle or hump in the beginning of anything, the rest of the work becomes easier and more doable.

There are plenty of books on this subject on the market, thanks again for choosing this one! Every effort was made to ensure it is full of as much useful information as possible, please enjoy!

Chapter 1: How Much Money Is Enough? Investing in Real Estate on the Cheap

One of the most basic concepts that you need to first understand about investing in real estate has to do with money. While it would be nice if I could sit here and right about how you don't need much money in order to invest in real estate, this is often not the case. I would be lying to you if I told you this; however, there are still ways that you can begin to get your finances in order so that eventually you can be in a position where you can purchase a chunk of what the real estate investment market has to offer. Again, once you get over the initial hump of investing in your first place, these types of endeavors often become easier to manage because you have more disposable income at your fingertips. This chapter will look at the types of things you should be doing in order to prime yourself to purchase real estate or invest in a piece of real estate. It's important to understand first that the younger you are, the easier time you will have figuring out the real estate investment market because you'll have more time to save money and make mistakes; however, even if you're someone who is older and is just starting to become interested in real estate investing, these tips are sure to also put everything in better perspective for you.

Why Having Good Credit is Important

Prior to 2008, it seemed like the banks would literally allow anyone to purchase a loan for a huge house with a massive backyard to match. Now that the bubble has popped and reality has hit thousands of Americans who have realized the dangers of purchasing expensive properties that have colossal mortgages attached to them, people are starting to realize the importance of having enough capital up front before purchasing a property. One other thing that the mortgage lenders have largely stopped doing is offering people with bad credit more money than they can afford, and they have also largely stopped giving people money with huge interest rates attached to them. Instead of creating an unsustainable situation for yourself, it's important to start establishing good credit now. It's going to be much harder to find a bank who will issue you a loan for a rental property or a flip property if your credit is under 700. Plus, if you have low credit and are still offered a loan, you are going to have a high interest rate that's attached to the loan itself, and this is going to force you to pay the bank more money than you would otherwise have to. While it is beyond the scope of this book to detail ways that you can establish good credit for yourself, if you are someone who is suffering from the impact of a bad or low credit score, figure out what you need to do to get your credit score at or above the 700 range. This will save you money before you start investing in any type of real estate venture.

How Much Does My Down Payment Need to Be?

It's safe to say that if you're young, two of the best ways to purchase your first real estate investment property is to either purchase a single-family home and live in it while you move through the process of flipping it, or purchase a multi-family home, rent one side of it out and live in the other half while you save money to flip your next property. Of course, these tactics are mostly used when people are looking to start real estate investing full-time. While both of these plans are sound in theory, the reality is that they also cost a good chunk of change. While we are certainly going to have a more in-depth discussion about how you can successfully flip a property, the first thing that you need to know about are the finances. This is where the idea of a loan and a down payment come into play. Unless you have more than $75,000 at your disposal just waiting to be spent, it's more than likely that you're going to need to take out a loan in order to purchase the house that you are looking to buy. In addition to taking out a loan, there is also the pesky down payment that you need to consider. You are able to put down as little as five percent of the entire price of the property on a house that you're looking to flip; however, this type of decision is actually going to cost you more in the long-term.

The general consensus for almost all mortgage loans is that if you put down less than twenty percent that is owed on the overall house, you are going to also have to purchase mortgage insurance because you look like a flight risk compared to someone who has put down more money. When you put down at least twenty percent of the entire cost of the property down in the form of a down payment, this is known as a thirty-year fixed mortgage. As you begin to look at property that you want to invest in, you should take note of the price of each one. After you have found a financial range within you have decided to operate, take twenty percent of this range number so that you can figure out how much money you need in order to put a down payment on this type of property. Remember, the less money the house costs, the more work that is going to need to be done on the property. Once you purchase the home, are you going to be able to finance the renovations that are needed in order to flip the property? It's important to ask yourself these questions prior to purchasing the house. Cheap houses are cheap for a reason. In the real estate world, nothing ever comes cheap without evidence as to why this is so.

What if I don't want to Flip a Property?

Truth be told, flipping a property is one of the more expensive ways to invest in real estate, although if you live in the property that you're flipping you'll be able to make up for some of this cost. Again, if you decide to purchase a multi-family property instead of buying a single -family property, it's also likely that you will not be paying any of your mortgage at all each month; your tenant will do that for you. Still, after you crunch your numbers and figure out that you won't have the capital to invest in an entire property on your own for several years, you still have some options. Two of the cheaper ways to invest in real estate without actually purchasing an entire property for yourself are real estate investment trusts and real estate investment groups. While we are going to discuss each type of investment trust and group in more detail in another chapter, it's important to first understand that these are the cheaper ways to invest in real estate before we move into how you exactly invest in each one in the first place. The cheaper of these two options is the real estate investment trust, which focus on investing in commercial real estate. Generally speaking, you only need between $500 to $2,500 to begin investing in this manner. If you have more capital than this and are looking to see greater returns on your investment, your next option would be to invest with a real estate investment group. These types of groups are privatized in nature, and essentially build properties for other landlords to purchase and rent out on their own. Again, we will get into the details of how a real estate investment group operates in a different chapter. The important thing to understand right now is that it costs between $5,000 to $50,000 to invest in a real estate investment group. Obviously, this is a wide range, so you have plenty of options here.

This chapter should have given you the information that you need in order to understand how much money you need in order to start investing in real estate. To recap, the first thing that you need to make sure is that you have a good credit score, especially if you're going to be buying a home and flipping it for rent. After you've established that you have an adequate credit score, the next step is to decide which type of investment you're going to participate in. This largely depends on how much capital you have, which is why we went into the financial details of three different types of real estate investment strategies right from the jump. The range of money that you need to have in order to invest in real estate ranges from a mere $500 to a whopping $50,000. You should be able to figure out where you fall quite easily depending on your personal financial situation. Understanding how much money you need is the first step towards investing in real estate. Thus, this first step is relatively straightforward in nature.

Chapter 2: How to Flip a House with No Money

Now that you have a basic understanding of the various types of real estate investment strategies that are at your disposal, the next step is to understand how to get started within each one. Of course, it's safe to say that most people want to purchase and flip a home using as little of their own personal money as they possibly can, and if you're looking to do this through conventional means, you may not be as successful as you hope you could be. This chapter is going to look at how you can flip a property with as little money as possible, and this is typically done through the purchase of a foreclosed home. We will look at both the advantages and disadvantages that exist when purchasing a foreclosed home, as well as tips on how to do this the right way and as cheaply as possible. If you are not interested in purchasing a foreclosed home and are instead interested in purchasing a home that is simply being sold on the market, much of the advice in this chapter will still apply to you as well.

What is a Foreclosure

A foreclosure is a situation that occurs when a homeowner does not pay his or her mortgage for a long period of time. When a homeowner cannot pay his or her mortgage, this debt does not simply go away. Instead, it accrues and collects as debt against the homeowner. It's important to understand that in this situation, the "homeowner" is more of a "home borrower". If you cannot pay your mortgage payments, then you no longer own the home. You are borrowing the home from the bank at this point. A foreclosure is a legal procedure that gives possession of the property officially over to the institution that initially provided a loan to the individual, and this institution is more likely that not a bank. It costs the lending institution a lot of money in order to pay for the entire foreclosure process, which is why it's typically advised that a person who cannot make their mortgage payments should alert their lending institution as soon as possible. The major reasons why people end up being unable to pay their loans usually include life hardships such as divorce, health, death or unemployment. Anyway, this is of no importance to you. You are just looking to purchase the property, without having to worry about the unfortunate circumstances that are surrounding why the home is being foreclosed in the first place.

The process of a foreclosure will begin between three to six months after a borrower has consistently not paid his or her mortgage for one reason or another. At this point, the lender will issue what is sometimes referred to as a Notice of Default, or a NOD for short. Wherever the home is located, their county record's office is notified of this situation, and this record goes public. In some states, the lender is also required to post an official notice on the door of the home. This gives the owner some heads up that his or her home is in danger of being taken by the lending institution. This is a warning notice, and it is intended to tell the borrower, "Hey, if you don't figure something out, you are going to lose the rights to this property." After the borrower receives this notice, he or she still has not officially lost the rights to the property. He or she will then enter a period of time known as "pre-foreclosure". Pre-foreclosure typically lasts between thirty to one-hundred and twenty days. During this time period the borrower is able to work out a negotiation with the lending institution so that the homeowner does not lose the home.

You may have heard of a "short-sale" before. A short-sale is when the borrower makes a deal with the lending institution during the pre-foreclosure period. During this time, the borrower is able to put the house up for sale at a price that is cheaper than what is owed on the property. In this way, the lending institution is "shorted" some money, which is why it is called a short sale. As someone who is purchasing the property, you may think that there is profit to be had from purchasing a short-sale because you are only spending money on the difference between what the borrower owes the bank. You're not actually purchasing the home at the full value of the property. While there is sense in purchasing a property in this manner as a buyer, there is also risk associated with it, which is why this book does not recommend purchasing a short-sale home, especially if this is your first go at real estate investing. Because a short sale is initiated during the pre-foreclosure period, there is no guarantee that a buyer is going to end up owning the property in question. The bank or lending institution certainly does not want to end up losing money on the property if they can help it, so if they can negotiate with the borrower before the home is sold via a short sale, they will most always do that. Another big reason why short-sale homes are not the best to buy is because it is generally a long, tiring, and drawn-out process.

The Foreclosure Buying Process

We could go into more details about how the foreclosure process works, but this information is not very useful to you, someone who is merely trying to purchase a property on the cheap. It should be fairly obvious that there are many details that go into purchasing a foreclosed property, and that not all real estate agents are prepared to help potential homeowners in this way. This is why the first step in the foreclosure purchasing process is to find a real estate agent who specializes in foreclosed homes. This type of institution will be able to guide you every step of the way during the foreclosure home purchasing process. They will also more than likely have a database of foreclosed homes that go beyond the regular homes that are found on a database like the MLS.

Step one and step two should be accomplished in close conjunction with each other. Step two is to find a lending institution who is going to complement the goals that you have and who is going to work closely with your specialized real estate agent. It would probably be a good idea to talk to the real estate agent you end up going with, because he or she most likely has a connection with a lender who also specializes in foreclosed homes. In most cases, it's important that you meet with a lender soon after you meet with the real estate agent. This will show both the real estate agent and the lending institution that you are serious about wanting to purchase a foreclosed property. After you've found both a lender and a real estate agent, the next step is one that is the same as when you purchase a regular home. You will need a preapproval letter from your mortgage lender, stating that you are going to be borrowing a predetermined amount of money for a predetermined period of time. An important tip here is to keep in mind that the institution who is lending money to the borrower who can no longer pay their mortgage is more than likely not going to be interested in helping you finance this endeavor. Often, you will have to find an outside lender who will be willing to work with you and the bank in question.

The next step is to negotiate with the lending institution who is looking to sell the foreclosed property on the market. There are generally two factors that you need to keep in mind as you move through this process. The first one is that the sales price that the bank is going to offer is going to be largely dependent upon what other foreclosed homes in the area are being priced at. If you are looking to negotiate this price, you are going to want to do some independent research on your own first. The second important factor regarding negotiation tactics is to realize that you are most likely not going to receive a repair discount from the bank. When you purchase a home that is not being foreclosed, you are able to negotiate with the seller so that you don't have to do unnecessary repairs yourself. For example, if the bathtub looks like it's about to crash through the floor that it's sitting in and has a lot of rust on it, you can request that the tub be replaced prior to purchasing the home. If you have someone come in and do a home inspection, you can request that areas of mold are removed from the home prior to your agreement to purchase. Factors like this are often not considered when you purchase a foreclosed home. You are getting a deal because you are purchasing the property at a cheaper rate than you would otherwise be able to grab it. Due to this fact, you are expected to purchase the home as-is.

Outlined above were the basic factors that you need to consider when deciding to purchase a foreclosed home. If you follow these guidelines and take the advice of both your lending institution and your real estate agent, you are more likely to see success. Every foreclosure situation tends to be a unique situation, and due to this fact, there is no cookie-cutter amount of money that you're going to need in order to successfully purchase a home. Regardless, you are still going to want to put down twenty-percent of the price of the home so that you can guarantee yourself a lower interest rate and a thirty-year fixed rate mortgage plan. If the overall price of the house is less than normal because of the fact that it's a foreclosed home, this means that your down payment is going to be smaller as will your monthly mortgage payments. This is why purchasing a foreclosed home should be considered. Even if it means you will be giving yourself a headache in the short-term due to the mundane details that exist within a foreclosure deal, the money that you're saving is worth it in the long-term.

Chapter 3: Mistakes to Avoid When Flipping a House

Now that you have a broad understanding of how you can go about purchasing a house to flip, the process does not come to a halt. Instead, this chapter is going to inform you about the common mistakes that people make when they're looking to begin their house flipping lifestyle. Understanding and recognizing these mistakes will help you to not make these mistakes yourself when it comes time for you to get going on your first house flipping project. You may have already considered some of these potential mistakes that are out there, but you may have also not given these factors any consideration at all thus far. Let's take a look at some of these mistakes and how you can avoid them now.

Flipping a House Mistake 1: Not Enough Money

When you're doing your primary research about how much money you need in order to purchase a property that you're going to flip, it's not enough to simply think about the down payment. You're going to want to also consider other factors including taxes, inspection fees, and most importantly the cost of repair. If you're more of the business type and not really the hands-on repairman or repairwoman type, you are more than likely going to have to contract the repairs that you need to get done to other people. Depending on how many repairs need to be done, your budget for repair costs can add up quite quickly. In order to prevent a situation where you're sitting around waiting for your next paycheck from your daytime job (if you've decided not to make real estate investing a full-time job), you should be budgeting your expenditures before you even purchase your first property. A good idea is to find a range of money that will allow you to repair what you need to repair without being able to finance it. There's no use in owning a property that you're going to flip if you can't afford to pay for the flipping aspect of it, yet there seem to be too many aspiring homeowners who don't think about this until they've already bought the home in question.

Flipping a House Mistake 2: Not Enough Time

Flipping a house takes a lot of time, and many real estate investors do not consider this before they purchase a property to flip. Even before you buy the property that fits your financial and business needs, it can sometimes take months to find a home that meets your unique credentials. Once you have found a home, the negotiating process to buy the property can also take months, and this is especially true if you are looking for a discount and are purchasing a home that is foreclosed. There are codes that need to be met, and inspections that need to be undergone. This too, takes a lot of time. Once you have finally purchased the property, you need to invest even more time into the proper repairs. If you haven't properly budgeted, this can prove to be quite difficult. After you have the house just the way you want it, the next step is to find someone who will either rent or buy the home outright at a cost that's more expensive than the cost you purchased it at. If you don't budget your time correctly, you could end up sitting on the house much longer than you originally anticipated. When time is money, this is most likely something that you would rather not do.

Flipping a House Mistake 3: You're Not Handy Enough

If you have to contract all of the work that needs to be done on the house, you're going to be spending a small fortune on fixing it up and this does not bode well for your profit margin. This is often the reason why handymen will invest their time and energy into flipping property, and this is known in the business as "sweat equity". If you're someone who is naturally good at putting up drywall, laying tile, and installing products that need to be done by a plumber, then you are going to be saving money on the cost that it would otherwise take to have a professional come in and do this for you. If you don't have the skillset to take on these types of tasks, the next best thing is to develop an arsenal of people who will accomplish these tasks for you on the cheap. Often, if you can guarantee these types of people that you will have consistent work for them to do over a long period of time, they will be more likely to offer you some sort of deal in exchange for their services.

Flipping a House Mistake 4: Not Knowing Enough About the Market

One of the biggest mistakes that a beginner house flipper can make is choosing to purchase a home in a market that he or she knows nothing about. Sure, if you have the capital to do so it might be a great idea to invest in a property in New York City, but if you decide to purchase a home in Queens when the new hot spot for homebuying and renting is Brooklyn, then it's safe to say that you're going to realize sooner rather than later that you've made a bad decision. On the other hand, when you purchase a property in a location that is closely familiar to you, you will have a better idea of the prices for that given area as well as better information on the neighborhoods themselves. Let's look at an example. Say that you bought a home at a foreclosure sale of $60,000. This seems like a fabulous investment, right? Well, after you purchased the property, you come to realize how expensive the repairs on the home are going to truly be. The previous homeowner left the place in shambles, and after you do all of the repairs, you ultimately figure out that you have spent $25,000 in repair costs. This brings your total renovation and property purchase to be about $85,000. Ultimately, you figure out that you want to sell the house instead of rent it. You're tired, and you have decided that the real estate investment experience is not at all what you thought it would be. Unfortunately, you did not do your research on the properties surrounding the home prior to purchasing it either. It turns out that most of these homes go for roughly $85,000, which is the same price that you ended up spending on the property after renovation costs were calculated. In the end, you break even instead of making a profit, and you walk away from this experience wondering how you could have been so ignorant in the first place. This example should be enough to convince you to take the time to understand your market before you dish out any money in any shape or form.

Flipping a House Mistake 5: You Don't Consider an Exit Strategy Before Purchasing the Home

The last mistake that many newbie house flippers make is that they do not properly plan their exit strategy. Often what happens is that these new real estate investors get caught up in the process of purchasing the home and they forget that their ultimate goal is to make money on the property in question. Instead of waiting until you're ready to either sell or rent the property out, you need to ask yourself some basic questions. These types of questions include:

> 1. Ideally, what would the best-case scenario be regarding this property and your exit strategy goals?

> 2. If your ideal exit strategy does not come to fruition, what is the next-best scenario?

> 3. If you are unable to rent out the property, will you be able to sell it at a price that is profitable?

These three basic questions will help you to begin your exit strategy even before you have purchased a property. Without an exit strategy, there's more of a likelihood that you're going to be holding onto your property for longer than is logical, and no aggressive real estate investor wants that. Hopefully this chapter has provided you with sound information on common mistakes that new real estate investors make, as well as information on preventative action that you can take so that you don't find yourself in a similar situation as the ones described here.

Chapter 4: Real Estate Investment Trusts and How They Work

Now that you understand how to flip a property on the cheap and the most common mistakes that many new house flippers make, we are going to turn attention away from flipping properties and broaden our understanding of real estate investing to include other aspects of the industry. This chapter will consider the topic of the real estate investment trust. As was already stated in the first chapter, investing into a real estate investment trust is one of the cheaper ways to invest in real estate altogether, so if you're someone who likes the idea of flipping a property but do not think that you'll have enough capital to do so in the near future, a real estate investment trust venture may just be perfect for you. To reiterate, people who invest in REITs typically will begin by investing anywhere between $500 to $2,500 dollars. Let's take a look what an REIT is, before heading into the details about how you can go about participating in one.

How Can a Real Estate Investment Trust be Best Defined?

A real estate investment trust is most commonly referred to as an REIT. An REIT is essentially a commercial, rather than a residential, type of real estate investment, and an REIT typically owns property where the entity that is renting the property is also earning income. Some popular types of structures that are owned by REITs include hotels, warehouses, hospitals, and shopping plazas. REITs are not typically interested in selling their property in the short term. Rather, these entities will hold onto the buildings that they

23

purchase and will see regular dividends come back to them through the rent that the business who is operating the property is paying. Besides the fact that REITs are a relatively cheap way to get started on the real estate investment market, another factor that makes them so popular is the idea that the income that is earned through these avenues can be tax-deductible. This is a great perk for any investor, and if you're someone who is typically fed up with the fact that government is always taking money from you, then this is one additional reason why an REIT is an attractive real estate investment option.

How to Join a Real Estate Investment Trust

While it's not really that expensive to participate with an REIT, the reality is that it would help you to have some experience on the stock market if you're looking to invest your money in this way. If you have never invested on the stock market before, the first step in this process is to find a stock broker. You see, not just anyone is able to take their money and gamble it away on the stock market. Only brokers who are certified to trade in this way can do so. In exchange for their services, a broker will charge you a brokerage fee, and will sometimes also charge you a commission fee based on the earnings that you make. It's important to calculate these fixed fees into your stock market budget prior to investing in an REIT, because if you don't the extra expense may come to surprise you when you're ready to cash out.

There are a few types of REITs that you are able to choose from on the stock market. These include stock exchange-listed REITs, REIT mutual funds, and exchange traded funds. Let's briefly look at what each of these different types of REITs can offer you as an investor on the stock market.

1. **Stock Exchange-Listed REITs:** These types of REITs are registered with the Securities and Exchange Commission (SEC), meaning that they are publicly traded on the stock market. When you see these types of REITs on the market, the price of a share of one of them will likely vary from day-to-day, depending on what the share price is for a particular period of time. It's also important to note that the majority of REITs that exist are publicly traded on the stock market in some way shape or form.

2. **REIT Mutual Funds:** An REIT mutual fund operates in the same way as a nondescript mutual fund does, so it's important that you fully understand what a mutual fund is. A mutual fund is a group where money is pulled together that is collectively owned by many different individual investors. REIT mutual funds are a large reason why individual investors are able to purchase shares of a commercial property more cheaply than if they were to purchase the building outright themselves. A mutual fund is managed by a professional financial advisor, who makes decisions for the group based on their shared interests.

3. **Exchange Traded Funds:** Exchange traded funds trade similarly to mutual funds, but with one clear difference. Exchange traded funds, or ETFs, are able to be traded on the stock exchange, whereas mutual funds are not always traded in this manner. Additionally, most ETFs will track some sort of index over the course of the day, and this index will allow the funds to either appreciate or depreciate depending on the goals of the collective funds.

Types of REITs

Now that we have looked at some of the different possibilities that are available to you in terms of trading your REIT on the stock market, we are now going to look at some of the different types of REITs that you can invest in from a physical building perspective. These REITs include retail, residential, healthcare, and even mortgage.

REIT Type 1: Retail

If you live anywhere that is mildly populated, it's more than likely that you yourself have shopped at an REIT without even knowing it. Retail REITs include shopping plazas, strip malls, and even malls. The property along these plazas and malls are divided so that space can be given to many store owners at the same time. Once an REIT has invested in this space by giving money to build the space up front, they can then charge their shop owners rent each month to ensure that they will see monthly returns on their investment. If you invest in the construction of a huge shopping mall, it's safe to assume that the cost of that mall is going to be quite large. On the other hand, once you have found shop owners and corporations who are looking to rent out these spaces that are within the mall, you are going to collectively receive income from every single one of them. The more money you provide up front for the construction of this project, the larger the returns are going to be for your wallet over the long term.

REIT Type 2: Residential

Residential REITs can include either multi-family homes or also apartment complexes or condominiums. In order for a residential REIT to be successful and worthy of your time and money, it is almost mandatory that you find a residential REIT in an area where the cost of rest is higher than compared to the rest of the country. For example, if you were to invest in an REIT in the Silicon Valley, you would want to make sure that you pick a place where the rent is high (which it certainly is in the Silicon Valley). You would also want to make sure that there are many young people flocking there who are looking to rent an apartment because they simply cannot afford the high costs associated with purchasing a home in that area. If you choose to engage in a residential REIT where the cost of buying a house is comparable to renting one, you will likely lose business to people who have decided that it's more convenient to buy a home instead of rent one.

REIT Type 3: Healthcare REIT

Healthcare REITs invest in construction projects for hospitals, urgent care centers, and even retirement communities. With the healthcare industry on a seemingly eternal climb towards profitability and relevance, it's safe to assume that this type of REIT is a profitable one in which to invest your money. The ways that these types of REITs make their money include the cost of private client medical bills, insurance premiums, and government services such as Medicaid and Medicare. Of course, the constant changes in the United States healthcare system might be one reason to caution against investing in this type of REIT; however, the healthcare industry as a whole seems to be finding profit nonetheless, so you should invest in this type of REIT at your own personal discretion.

REIT Type 4: Mortgage REIT

The last type of REIT at which we're going to look are REITs that are tied to huge conglomerate mortgage companies such as Freddie Mac and Fannie Mae. These companies are big, and their size can contribute to more risk being involved in your investment. If you're someone who does not generally trust large corporations (much less large corporations who were previously indicated in the 2008 financial crisis), then it might be best to stay away from these types of institutions. If you are someone who has experience in working with corporations, then a mortgage REIT might be something from which you will be able to benefit.

This chapter may have been boring to you in the sense that it was loaded with information pertaining to the stock market and the specific types of REITs that are available to you, but this was not done by mistake. Investing in an REIT is relatively simple in the sense that you find a broker who will provide you with what you need to make investments are your leisure. The tough part is the research aspect of investing in an REIT, which is why you need as much information as you can get regarding each specific type of REIT that's out there. REITs contrast flipping houses in the sense that there are many things that are done behind the scenes when you're working in an REIT. When you're flipping a house, things are much more transparent. The good news is that if you're investing in an REIT, you're going to be spending a lot less money than if you decided to purchase a property and flip it. If you were to lose $500 due to inadequate research, yes it would negatively influence your investment portfolio, but it's only $500. When compared to $20,000 or more, $500 is only a drop in the bucket, which is why an REIT can seem pretty attractive to a new real estate investor at the end of the day.

Chapter 5: Real Estate Investment Groups and How They Differ from Trusts

This chapter is going to focus on another type of investment strategy that differs from the real estate investment trust strategy that we previously discussed in the last chapter. We will be focusing on what exactly a real estate investment group is and how to join one. We will also focus some of our attention on some of the key differences that exist between real estate investment groups and real estate investment trusts. If you recall from the first chapter, the amount of money that you will need in order to invest in a real estate investment group (REIG), can range between $500 to $50,000. You may be wondering why this range is so large. After reading this chapter, you will likely have a better understanding as to why this is so. This chapter will also contain some details about the pros and cons to joining an REIG.

A real estate investment group is also sometimes referred to as a private partnership. Instead of simply engaging in stock exchanges over the internet or with a broker, an REIG looks to invest in building their own property and then selling it to a landlord who will take care of interacting with the tenant on a more frequent basis. You have probably seen these types of homes before. There will be a group of condominiums that are being built in your neighborhood, or a ritzy apartment complex where the homes are actually detached from one another. These are the types of home that REIGs are likely to build. The REIG promises to find the tenants for the landlord in question, as well as resolve most of the maintenance issues that arise on the property. In return, the landlord will agree to give a portion of the tenant's rent pay to the REIG, and this is what the investors within the REIG will see as profit. The biggest advantage that an REIG can offer a real estate investor is the opportunity to own a property without the hassle of having to interact with a tenant. The biggest point that has to be made also about how these investors interact with the landlord often involves a vacancy clause. While the real estate investors will pay for repairs and the initial cost to build the property, they will often not agree to pay for any property vacancy that the landlord may experience. The REIG wants their monthly portion of the tenant's rent each and every month, regardless of whether or not there is actually an individual or a family residing in the home. When this happens, it is up to the landlord to find a way to get them their money.

When the group is paid in an REIG, often there will be a manager who is controlling and operating the funds within this pooled effort. In this way, REIGs sometimes work the same way that mutual funds do, because the members of the REIG even agree to sign what's known as a prospectus before engaging in any REIG activity. A prospectus is basically a document that states that the money manager is going to manage the group's money in a predetermined way that has already been agreed upon by each member of the group. This way, there is no confusion about whether or not the money manager is working in the best way possible. In an REIG, your money is definitely working in a team-oriented way. If you're someone who does not mind having slightly decentralized control of your money, then an REIG might be perfect for you.

Why Should You Consider Investing in an REIG?

The biggest reason why investors will think about and eventually join an REIG is the fact that they don't have to spend as much money as they would if they were to go into business with themselves. This is a collective effort with the entire group who owns the property within it. Another financial reason why someone might end up joining an REIG is that there is a money manager who is on their side and who is making sure that things make sense from a financial perspective. If you're someone who sometimes forgets to look at things financially and you have the tendency to approach a situation and say, "eh, I'll make it happen" without giving much practical thought to it, then this would be another reason why you should invest in an REIG.

Moving away from the financial benefits of joining an REIG, another benefit that does not have to do much with money is the idea that as an investor in an REIG, you still have the ability to see a property being built and interact with the process in this way. For example, in an REIT, there is less of an ability to actually see the fruits of your investment because you are often behind a computer or with a broker when these transactions are being conducted. You are unable to actually see the property that your money helped to build. Sometimes pride is one of the reasons why people decide that they want to invest in real estate, and this factor should not be thrown to the wayside. When you can walk down the sidewalks of a neighborhood and tangibly see your success, it's a great feeling. In addition to this reality, if you are someone who simply is not a people person, you should consider joining an REIG. When you invest in an REIG, you don't need to interact with tenants on a daily basis. You're away from the drama that can sometimes ensue with tenants, and this can be a source of anxiety that is pushed further from yourself. This also brings up another great point. When you're investing in real estate (or going into any business venture), you want to make sure that your actions are coinciding with your own personal feelings and characteristic makeup. If you hate interacting with people, why would you decide to be a landlord? These are the types of character-related questions that you should be asking yourself during this process, so that you can ultimately decide which type of investment strategy is going to work best for you.

Now that we have talked about the pros of investing in an REIG, it's time to give the cons some consideration. Probably the biggest disadvantage that an REIG can offer to a prospective investor is that sometimes these groups will actually charge their members money each month for being part of the group. If you are someone who can afford to pay fifty-dollars each month for this type of investment group, then that's fine; however, there are some groups who charge as much as two-hundred dollars per month if you want to be a part of their group. For someone who is looking to invest in real estate on the cheap, this may be a rather large deterrent for you. Of course, not every group is like this. There are REIGs that do not charge a monthly group fee at all. Be sure to do some research on the price of joining an REIG in your area before immediately discarding this investment option. Additionally, another negative aspect of joining an REIG has to do with the concept of time. Meetings for REIGs often take a few hours of you time. Each group will have their own parameters in terms of how often they decide to meet. If your group meets once or twice a month, you want to make sure that you have this time available in your schedule before committing to this investment strategy. If you have kids, you want to make sure that this meeting does not interfere with extracurricular activities that they're also pursuing. Lastly, there is a sense of competition that can exist within an REIG. You're opening yourself up to people whom you've never met, and you all have the same goal of making money. If you're not careful, you could end up unknowingly lining the pockets of someone who is in your same "group", because of information that you have about the market that they may not know. Of course, when you're first starting out in real estate investing, it's likely that these people are going to have more information than you and you can use this fact to your benefit; however, as you become more experience keep in mind that this line of thinking goes both ways.

Hopefully this chapter has provided you with yet another option to add to your investment options. Generally speaking, REIGs can be a great way for new investors to get their foot in the door and learn from people who have been in the industry for quite some time. It's also important to recognize that sometimes the people who newly enter an REIG do not even begin to invest in anything before they have learned from their peers. One of the fastest ways to become well acquainted with any market really is to find a mentor. Joining an REIG will allow you to meet with people in an industry in which you're interested. If you can form trusting relationships with these people, you'll be able to see them work and learn from them through experience. Experience is often a priceless tool to have, especially when every industry these days typically requires a lot of it in order for success to be had.

Chapter 6: Tips and Tricks to Consider when Investing in Real Estate

Now that you have a working understanding of some of the various types of real estate investment strategies that you can choose from, this next chapter is going to discuss some of the top tips and tricks that real estate investors use when they're looking to enter the real estate investment market with a new property or investment in their possession. It's important to understand that many of these tips and tricks can be applied to all three types of investment strategies at which we've looked, and this has to do largely with the real estate investment market as a whole. For example, when you decide to invest in a real estate investment trust or a real estate investment group, you may think that you are simply handing your money over to someone who is going to know what to do with it. The situation is largely out of your hands. If this is your mentality, then you may never be a great real estate investor. At the end of any money chain involved in the real estate investment marketplace is a building of some kind. This building should meet certain criteria in your head about what makes a good investment property. If you are simply handing over your money for someone else to control, without taking the time that's necessary to investigate the way in which your money is handled, how are you going to know and be able to control the type of property that you're purchasing? This chapter is going to focus on tips and tricks that great real estate investors use so that they know when they're making a good deal and when they're looking at buying a lemon.

Real Estate Investing Top Trick 1:
Find the Worst House in the Best Neighborhood

One of the mantras that you have probably heard time and again is "location, location, location" regarding real estate. This idea still holds true to this day, and as an aspiring investor it would behoove you to recognize this fact as quickly as possible. Of course, this certainly does not mean that every new investor should be looking to invest in expensive high rise apartments in New York City. You're an investor who is looking to invest with as little money as possible. How do expect to do that? A great tip that many investors use is that they will look for the worst house in the best neighborhood. Why? Because it provides the investor with the opportunity to build equity on the property. Equity in the real estate world can be best defined as the market value of the property minus the mortgage money that is still due on the property by the borrower. The logic is that if you're purchasing a home that is cheaper than the other ones in the neighborhood, then your mortgage is also going to be comparably cheaper. In addition to this fact, when you work on the property through the repairs that you're going to be making on it, this will raise the price of the home when you go to sell it.

Real Estate Investing Top Trick 2:
Find the Best Neighborhood

The first tip requires us to think about what qualities the "best" neighborhood possesses when we're looking to purchase a property either to rent out or to flip and sell. This type of thinking does not just apply to a situation where you buy a home outright, either. If you are thinking about investing in an REIT or an REIG instead of flipping a house on your own, this logic can still apply to you as you look for places

35

to build and invest that make logical sense. When experienced real estate investors look for properties in which they're going to put their money, they often will divide the different neighborhoods into three categories. These categories do not have fancy names; rather they are simply delineated as neighborhood type A, neighborhood type B, and neighborhood type C. Neighborhood A contains neighborhoods that are extremely nice, maybe too nice, for someone who is looking to flip a property. The people who live in these types of homes are usually moms and dads. They have kids, mini vans, and white picket fences. These types of people are typically looking to buy a home through the most traditional means that they can. While flipping a property is not quite considered to be unconventional these days, there are also more conventional ways that homes can be bought.

Neighborhood type B contains properties that are usually just what an aspiring real estate investor is looking for. This type of neighborhood contains a lot of blue collar families. You can often tell that this is the case by the white working vans that are usually parked outside. Another indicator that you're in a blue-collar neighborhood is if you see a lot of pickup trucks with tools piled into them, or people who have their own lawn mowing service. Often, this type of property is a great place to invest in as a new real estate investor because of the fact that these families are more likely to rent property than buy it themselves. Also, this type of neighborhood gives you more flexibility because it's unlikely that anyone is going to become angered by your presence there. For example, let's say that you decide to purchase a single-family home in a type A neighborhood. You then decide to take this single-family home and convert it into a multi-family home so that you can eventually rent it out and have two tenants living there instead of one. While this does indeed sound great for your wallet, the problem with this scenario is that you are going to be unintentionally giving people the opportunity to live in a type A neighborhood without them having to actually afford it in full themselves. This may anger some of the people who live in the type A neighborhood, people who are well off and like to see things in a very limited light. When you purchase a property in a type B neighborhood instead of a type A neighborhood, it's more likely that there will be other investors in the area, so you will lower your chances of angering anyone in the community. You will also more than likely see other investors working alongside of you in this type of neighborhood, trying to make a buck just like you are.

Neighborhood type C is reserved for those properties that are located in places that are a bit on the unpredictable side. In these types of neighborhoods, crime might be an issue, or the school system in this particular area might be less than ideal. For these reasons, only experienced real estate investors typically find themselves going into these neighborhoods to make a profit. Other problems that sometimes occur within these types of neighborhoods include situations where the tenants destroy the contents of the home and then leave the home. You're left with picking up the repair bill with little to no hope of seeing anymore rent from these people ever again. These are the types of problems that can occur when you decide to invest in real estate in a C type neighborhood. If you don't know what you're doing in these areas, there's a chance that you will get swindled out of your money or potentially worse. If you're a new investor, your best bet is to stick with B type neighborhoods when you can.

Real Estate Investing Top Trick 3:
Remember Your Tax Benefits

Too often I hear about real estate investors who seem to be doing well, but who forget to take their tax benefits into account when they go to file their taxes. One of the biggest reasons why the United States government provides tax write offs to real estate investors is because they know that if these individuals (like you and me) weren't buying and selling properties, they would have to be the only supplying it for thousands of people. Make sure that you look into arguably the biggest write off that is available to you. This is known as the Depreciation Write-Off. Obviously, you will have to invest a small amount of money and time to talk to a tax specialist who can help you in these processes, but it is definitely worth it. If you are someone who did not calculate your tax benefits into your initial plan when you were first figuring out financing for your property, then you can expect more money than you originally anticipated. REITs and REIGs also offer tax benefits; these benefits are not exclusively for people who purchase property on their own. Be sure that you don't forget to look into this as you begin to invest in more and more properties.

Real Estate Investing Top Trick 4:
The Perks of the One Percent Rule

What's the point in purchasing an investment property if you're unable to make a profit from it? The purpose of the one percent rule is to make sure that you're making enough money from the property itself to make it worth your while in both the short and long-term. The one percent rule is calculated by taking the price of the entire property and taking one percent from this number. This number, ideally, should represent the monthly rent you are going to charge for living in the space. For example, let's say that you pay $175,000 for a duplex property. If you were going by the one percent rule, this would mean that you would have to charge a rent of $1,750 per month in order for this venture to make sense. After you have figured out this number, you then have to ask yourself some questions about the neighborhood where the property resides. Will you be able to charge this much rent for the property? If you are purchasing a multi-family home, you will more than likely be able to make this happen; however, if you're purchasing a single-family home where rent is relatively cheap, this may be more difficult. Take the time to think about how you're going to make money once you're done renovating the property. You'll save yourself frustration and time by thinking in this manner

Real Estate Investing Top Trick 5:
Understand and Value a Good Tenant

The last tip at which we're going to look is understanding and valuing a good tenant. There are horror stories out there, too many of them, about initially good tenants going bad and ruining a landlord's property. Taking the time to properly interview people who are potentially going to be living in a space that you largely renovated with your own hands and money is important. Once your tenant signs the dotted line on the lease, that living space is theirs for at least a year (typically). Signs of a good tenant include people who have been living on the property already for over ten years (if you're purchasing a duplex where people already live, for example), people with kids and a family because they're less likely to throw raging parties that last well into the wee hours of the morning, and older people over the age of fifty-five.

For all of the tips that were presented in this chapter, it's important to understand that not all of these tips always hold true, but for the most part they do. For example, I know someone who calculated the one percent rule, but also has fabulous tenants who simply cannot pay one percent of the price of the house each month. Instead of kicking these people out and making them find a new home, instead this savvy investor decided to strike a deal. The tenant in question was a landscaper and had expensive lawn equipment that he used on a regular basis for his business. Instead of increasing the rent, she simply wrote into the lease a clause where this family (mainly the father) is required to take care of the lawn each week. Lawn upkeep over the course of one year certainly isn't cheap, and this investor knew that she herself did not want to have to bother with mowing or weeding the yard. While she is not seeing one percent of her investment in the form of a monthly rent check, she is still seeing profit in a unique way. These situations do arise, so it's important to keep in mind that you might find yourself dealing with this type of scenario. Don't just throw these opportunities to be creative away because these tips are not listed within this chapter.

Conclusion

Thank for making it through to the end of *Real Estate Investing: Master the Skill of Real Estate Investing*, let's hope it was informative and able to provide you with all of the tools you need to achieve your goals whatever it may be. This book was meant to provide you with not just information, but also information on how you can take actionable steps towards reaching your real estate investment goals in the near future. With this information at your disposal, the metaphorical ball is now in your court. If you know that you need to save some more money before you start investing in the strategy that interests you the most, start there. While you're getting your finances in order, keep gaining a solid and foundational knowledge base that will take your ability to invest properly to the next level. Remember, no one said that real estate investing was going to be easy; however, if you properly prepare yourself prior to jumping into the real estate investment field, you'll better your chances of immediate success.

The next step is to continue your research on which real estate investment strategy interests you the most. If this is the first book that you're reading on the topic of real estate investing, it's safe to say that this information is not going to be enough. If you still don't know which specific strategy is right for you, maybe make a list of each real estate investment strategy in terms of which one interests you the most and go from there. Over time, the type of information towards which you're gravitating will reveal itself, and you'll ultimately know which type of real estate investment strategy is right for you. Don't sell yourself short. Take the time that you need to figure out which strategy is going to fit your budget and your lifestyle best and go from there. Remember, you don't have to follow the crowd either. Just because one strategy works well for someone else, that does not mean that it will necessarily work well for you. Get to know yourself and your preferences throughout this process. You'll end up thanking yourself in the long-term.

Finally, if you found this book useful in anyway, a review on Amazon is always appreciated!